TEEN
PREGNANCY

TEEN
PREGNANCY

BY KAREN LATCHANA KENNEY

CONTENT CONSULTANT
CARL MAZZA, DSW, LMSW,
ASSOCIATE PROFESSOR OF SOCIAL WORK
LEHMAN COLLEGE OF THE CITY
UNIVERSITY OF NEW YORK

Essential Library

An Imprint of Abdo Publishing | www.abdopublishing.com

www.abdopublishing.com

Published by Abdo Publishing, a division of ABDO, PO Box 398166, Minneapolis, Minnesota 55439. Copyright © 2015 by Abdo Consulting Group, Inc. International copyrights reserved in all countries. No part of this book may be reproduced in any form without written permission from the publisher. Essential Library™ is a trademark and logo of Abdo Publishing.

Printed in the United States of America, North Mankato, Minnesota
042014
092014

THIS BOOK CONTAINS RECYCLED MATERIALS

Cover Photo: Monkey Business Images/Shutterstock Images
Interior Photos: Monkey Business Images/Shutterstock Images, 2; SimmiSimons/iStockphoto, 6; Wave Break Media/Shutterstock Images, 9; John Bill/Shutterstock Images, 15; Lumb Stocks/Library of Congress, 16; J. Scott Applewhite/AP Images, 24; Shutterstock Images, 26, 66, 68; Thinkstock, 29, 37, 38, 53, 88; Jupiter Images/Thinkstock, 33; Kevin Wang/AP Images, 40; Travis Manley/Shutterstock Images, 48; Golden Pixels LLC/Shutterstock Images, 56; Patricia Marks/Shutterstock Images, 58; Eugenia-Petrenko/Shutterstock Images, 62; Peter Bernik/Shutterstock Images, 65; Creatas/Thinkstock, 70; Doug Menuez/Thinkstock, 72; Papa Bravo/Shutterstock Images, 76; Prakash Hatvalne/AP Images, 79; Kris Vandereycken/Shutterstock Images, 84; Paul Sancya/AP Images, 95

Editor: Jenna Gleisner
Series Designer: Becky Daum

Library of Congress Control Number: 2014932564

Cataloging-in-Publication Data

Kenney, Karen Latchana.
  Teen pregnancy / Karen Latchana Kenney.
    p. cm. -- (Essential issues)
  Includes bibliographical references and index.
  ISBN 978-1-62403-422-0
  1. Teenage pregnancy--Juvenile literature. 2. Youth--sexual behavior--Juvenile literature.
  I. Title.
  306.874--dc23

                                        2014932564

CONTENTS

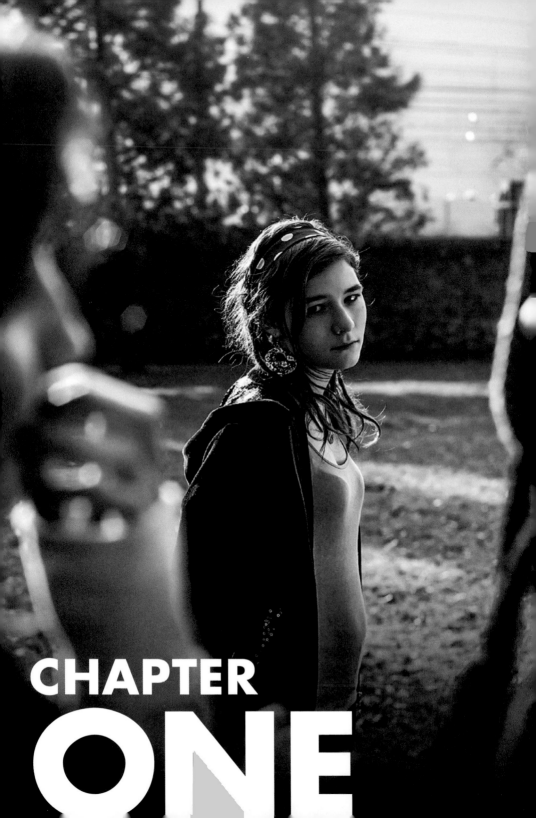

CHAPTER
ONE

KIDS HAVING KIDS

Sixteen-year-old Taylor Yoxheimer was in her junior year of high school. She played sports, hung out with her boyfriend, David, and basically enjoyed life. She never expected to be the pregnant girl at school, but she found out she was going to have a baby a few months after having unprotected sex with her boyfriend.

Taylor was devastated and hid her pregnancy from her parents for five months. She was afraid they would kick her out of the house. When they finally found out, Taylor's parents were so angry and disappointed they could barely look at her. As other students found out about the pregnancy, many stopped talking to Taylor or started making fun of her. Taylor's soccer team even said mean things to her. She lost many friends because of her pregnancy and felt others looked down on her because of her decision to have unprotected sex.

After a difficult and painful labor, Taylor gave birth to her son, David Jr. She was completely unprepared for

Teen pregnancy often results in ridicule and judgment from peers and older adults.

the difficulties of motherhood, and her world changed overnight: "I wish I would have known how hard it would be," she said. "Someone else's life depends on you. Having that kind of responsibility is SO stressful."[1] Taylor quickly learned losing sleep, changing diapers, and staying home instead of going out with friends were part of the exhausting job of being a teen mother. Taylor admits being a teen mom is difficult. Having children makes relationships more complicated. She and David Jr.'s father split up.

Teenage Pregnancy

Taylor is just one of many teens who give birth in the United States and around the world each year. Teens become pregnant for many reasons. Some long to be loved and think a baby will fill a void in their life. Others do not know how to prevent pregnancy or think it will not happen to them. And some think having a baby will strengthen their relationship with their partner. Many teens are unprepared for the realities of raising a child, though. They may quit school and find low-paying jobs to support their new family. Some teens survive only on welfare—governmental assistance issued to the poor or unemployed to pay for food, housing,

Teen pregnancy is the leading reason girls drop out of school.

and medical expenses. Sometimes, the cycle of poverty passes on to their children and new generations.

In developed countries, such as the United States, education is often the first sacrifice when a baby enters a high school student's life. It is incredibly difficult to finish homework and attend classes after staying up all night with a fussy baby. And if the mother does not have her family's support, she most likely has no one to watch her baby while she is at school. Having dropped out of school, many girls do not continue their education or earn their general equivalency degree (GED). In fact, less than 50 percent of teen mothers graduate from high school.[2] As a result, college is out of the question for many teen moms. Fewer than 2 percent graduate from college by the age of 30.[3]

Lacking education creates a vicious cycle of poverty that can be difficult to escape. Many employment doors close on teen moms who have not received high school or college degrees. Babies cost thousands of dollars each year—from diaper and food costs to doctor's appointments and day care. With needy babies and no income to buy the necessities, many teen moms and their babies survive on public assistance. Approximately 25 percent of teen moms go on welfare within three years after having a baby.[4] The financial burden of teen pregnancy then falls on taxpayers and government programs.

A teen father may be involved in his baby's life, but many teen fathers do not help with the daily care of their children. Just 20 percent of teen fathers marry their baby's mother, and the rest of the fathers must pay monthly child support.[5] Many teen fathers quit school and work in low-paying jobs. They pay an average of $800 each year in child support, which is based on their yearly earnings.

Not all teen parents decide to have and raise their children. Some other choices for pregnant teens are abortion or adoption. Approximately 35 percent of pregnant teens choose to abort their babies.[6] Abortion is a controversial issue affecting mothers of all ages. Some states have laws restricting a teen's access to abortions and require parent notification. Many teens are afraid

TEEN PREGNANCY STATISTICS IN THE STATES AND AROUND THE WORLD

Teen pregnancy rates are dropping in the United States. From 1991 through 2010, the rate of teen pregnancy dropped 44 percent. In 1970, 644,708 babies were born to teen mothers. In 2010, that number fell to 367,752 births.[7] While the rate for the country has dropped, not all states have had the same outcome. Some states, such as Arkansas and Mississippi, have very high teen birthrates, while other states, such as New Hampshire and Connecticut, have very low rates.

Despite its decline in the past few decades, the United States continues to have one of the highest teen pregnancy rates compared with similar developed countries. According to the United Nations Demographic Yearbook 2012, 41.5 of every 1,000 US teens ages 15 to 19 had children. In Canada, the teen birthrate was 14.1 out of every 1,000 teens. In France, the rate was 9.4, and in the Netherlands the rate was only 4.8.[8]

to tell their parents they are pregnant. These laws may cause some pregnant teens to seek out unsafe abortion options, which can have serious health consequences and even result in death. Fewer girls put their babies up for adoption. Less than 3 percent of teen parents choose adoption.[9]

Children of Teen Parents

As the child of a teen parent, life can result in hardship. Being born into poverty can lead to a cycle of poverty. Two-thirds of families started by poor, young, unmarried parents live in poverty.[10] Children of teen moms are more likely to perform poorly in school. Approximately 50 percent must repeat a grade.[11] They also are more likely to receive lower scores on standardized tests and not graduate high school. Later in life, daughters of teen moms are more likely to become teen moms as well, while sons are twice as likely to enter the prison system.[12]

Children born to teen mothers may have health problems. Many teen mothers do not receive proper prenatal health care, such as visiting the doctor regularly or taking vitamins important to fetus development. Some teens delay telling others they are pregnant and first visit a doctor in the later months of their pregnancy. They may contract sexually transmitted diseases (STDs), which can harm both their own health and the baby's health. STDs may cause premature birth, disease, or a low birth weight for the baby. These factors may then negatively affect a child's mental and physical development.

A Global Issue

While teen pregnancy is an issue in the United States, it is a much bigger issue in low- and middle-income countries. Approximately 16 million teen girls give birth around the world each year. In some of the poorest nations, nearly one in three girls give birth by the time they turn 18.[13]

More than 30 percent of girls in developing countries are married before the age of 18.[14] Many are not allowed

PRENATAL CARE

During a pregnancy, it is vital for the mother to abstain from alcohol, drugs, or tobacco, which can harm the fetus. Also, a mother needs to regularly visit the doctor to ensure she and the fetus are both in good health. Doctors check the baby's heartbeat and size, as well as the mother's blood pressure, weight, and other vital signs. Doctors also recommend childbirth classes so future parents can learn how to best take care of their newborn baby. Mothers also must take certain vitamins during their pregnancy to prevent illnesses and promote their baby's growth. Without the important monitoring done during prenatal care, babies are at a higher risk for developing health problems after they are born.

SEXUAL VIOLENCE

In some countries, sexual violence is very common. According to the WHO, nearly one-third of teenage girls are forced into their first sexual experience.[16] The results of rape include pregnancy, disease, and mental health issues. Child marriage is another form of sexual violence. It is legal for young girls to be married to older men in parts of Africa and South Asia. For example, it is common in some countries for girls to be married at the age of seven or eight. These young girls are forced into sexual relationships. They have little to no knowledge of sex, and their body is not yet sexually mature. This can result in long-term health problems.

or able to attend school and may have low educational levels. According to the World Health Organization (WHO), lower educational levels relate to higher birthrates, as many teens do not know about or have access to contraception. Also, sexual violence is widespread in developing countries. Teen girls are often unable to defend themselves against rape and become pregnant as a result. In some cultures, teen girls marry much older men and are forced into sexual relationships. In places with poor or nonexistent health-care systems, many teen girls die from pregnancy or childbirth. These are the leading causes of death for 15- to 19-year-old girls in low- and middle-income countries.[15] Stillbirths and infant deaths are also common for teen mothers from these nations.

Teen pregnancy is an issue affecting teens and societies around the world.

Teen pregnancy is an issue affecting more than teen parents and their babies. It also affects future generations who could be subjected to the poverty cycle. Education, abstinence, and access to contraceptives are some of the tools needed for prevention. Several government programs work to educate youth and support teen parents in the United States. And internationally, organizations strive to raise marriage ages, create awareness of sexual violence, and educate teens about preventing pregnancies. With more knowledge, teens have more options. They can make better choices to suit their life goals.

CHAPTER
TWO

CHANGING VIEWS ON TEEN PREGNANCY

Ages 12 and 14 may seem incredibly young to become a spouse or parent, but this perception has changed over time. Those ages were once considered the perfect time to get married and start a family. Early marriage and parenthood was once common and expected of many.

Historically, the average life-span was much shorter than it is now. Because of this, procreation had to begin earlier. Ancient Romans believed the appropriate marriage ages were 14 for males and 12 for females. Later, the Roman Catholic Church and much of Western Europe adopted these marriage ages. The ages were eventually written into English law and transferred to the United States with the colonists. These marriage laws stayed in effect until each state enacted new

In the mid-1800s, it was not uncommon for a young teen to marry and bear children.

A MAN'S PROPERTY

In ancient Rome, married men and women did not have equal legal rights. A man had legal rights over his wife and children; the wife and children were the husband's property. Women were not allowed to learn to write or be active in politics. Children could not own property if their father was still alive. Only the father of a Roman family could own property. He also decided if his newborn children would be allowed to stay in the family. Sometimes, deformed babies or babies born into poor families were abandoned outdoors if the father rejected them from the family.

laws concerning marriage. Americans questioned if 12- and 14-year-olds were prepared to become parents and face other marriage responsibilities. States began raising legal marriage ages, which now range from 15 to 21 years old, depending on the state.

In the Puritan and colonial times of the United States, adolescent girls were often married and had children. If an unwed girl became pregnant, she was quickly married. Becoming pregnant while unwed was viewed as socially unacceptable.

Through the 1950s, teen pregnancy was accepted in the United States as long as the girl was married when she became pregnant. Adoption and illegal abortions were alternative choices for unwed teens. The US teen birthrate hit its high in 1957, when 96 of every 1,000 teens had a child.[1] Teens gave up hundreds of thousands of babies for adoption from the mid-1940s to the mid-1970s. Most were closed adoptions, meaning the teen parents could not contact their children.

Starting in the 1960s, unwed teenage pregnancy became more of a visible social problem. Teen mothers began resisting marriages and even remained in school. From 1960 to 1975, there was a 50 percent increase in the number of children born to unwed teen mothers.[2]

"When my parents sent me to the Sophia Little Home in Cranston, RI, I was 17 and seven months pregnant by my boyfriend, a 19-year-old sailor. The youngest girl there was 14 and the oldest was 22. I spent the next two months doing arts and crafts. We were told not to tell each other our last names. We never talked about what was going to happen to our bodies. There was no help to prepare us for the grief that was to lie ahead."[3]
—Nancy Horgan, teen mother sent to a maternity home in 1968

Being Sent Away

Pregnant teens often hid their pregnancy from society. It was a shameful secret for an unwed, pregnant, teen mother's parents. People did not look down on the baby's father as much as the mother. Outsiders often thought the pregnancy was mostly the girl's fault. People expected respectable girls to abstain from sex until marriage, so sex education and contraception were rarely provided to teens.

Parents sent their young, unwed pregnant daughter to a maternity home just as she began showing her pregnancy. Maternity homes were places where pregnant girls lived until they delivered their children. Some homes only admitted girls who promised to give their child up for adoption. Keeping the baby was not an option. People labeled children of unwed mothers as "bastards," and many believed adoption to a good home could free a child from that social stigma.

Schools often expelled pregnant girls. These girls then had to attend school in maternity homes. They would go away for a few months and then return home without their babies. Their families would make up stories explaining their daughter's disappearance. For example, they would say the girl went to stay with a sick aunt or had an illness. Sometimes, the young fathers never even knew about the pregnancies. No one talked about it, and life went on as if nothing had ever happened.

In the 1970s, social stigma attached to unwed teen mothers began to lessen, as did the pressure to give up children for adoption. The decade opened up reproductive options for teens, allowing them more control over whether or not they wanted to become teen parents.

New Choices

In 1960, the birth control pill was approved for use in the United States. The pill prevents the release of eggs during a woman's menstrual cycle. It gives women the freedom to control their fertility. When the pill was first released, it was no longer only the man's decision to use contraceptives, such as condoms. Women could now choose whether or not to become pregnant. They could delay motherhood to pursue higher education and careers. It opened up a world of opportunities to women.

Before the late 1960s, it was illegal for doctors to prescribe the pill to unmarried girls younger than 21 without parental consent. In 1970, the Family Planning federal program was founded. This program funded family planning

BANNING SEX DISCRIMINATION IN SCHOOLS

In 1972, Title IX of the Education Amendments Act banned public schools from expelling pregnant teens. This law ensures pregnant and parenting teens have equal access to education. It also requires student excuses from school due to their pregnancy and childbirth. The law makes sure students are not forced to attend special schools for pregnant and parenting teens.

centers offering contraceptives and other reproductive health services to low-income individuals. In 1972, after the government reduced the voting age to 18, many states lowered the age of majority to 18. That meant girls 18 years and older no longer needed parental permission to get a prescription for the birth control pill. That year, it also became legal for unmarried women to take the pill. Before that time, doctors prescribed the pill only to married women. By 1974, many states lowered the age girls could start taking the pill without a parent's permission to 14 or 15. Though access to the drug was limited for years, it became an effective method of preventing teen pregnancy.

In 1973, another option for pregnant women became legal in the United States. The historic US Supreme Court decision in the *Roe v. Wade* case ruled women in all states had the right to an abortion if they wanted one during their first trimester. Before this decision, not all states allowed doctors to perform abortions. Many women sought out illegal and medically unsafe abortions to end their pregnancies. These abortions were risky, and many women died from the procedures. In 1965, 17 percent of women's deaths related to pregnancy and childbirth were the result of unsafe abortions. After abortions became legal, the risk of harm dropped dramatically. By 2006, it was less than 0.3 percent.[4]

Certain states enacted laws restricting unmarried minors access to abortions after the procedure became legal. The laws aimed to limit the number of abortions performed on teens in these states. In 2013, 44 states still had laws requiring parental consent or notification in order to perform an abortion.

Government Programs

In the 1970s, teen pregnancy was a big enough issue in the United States to gain the attention of the federal government. The Office of Adolescent Pregnancy

ILLEGAL ABORTIONS

By 1880, abortions were illegal in every US state. Despite this, a need existed for abortions, and they were available to women who sought them out. Since abortions were illegal, the government did not regulate the practice. Practically anyone could say they performed abortions. Some abortionists were doctors or midwives, but others had no medical training at all. This led to harmful practices resulting in infertility, infection, and death. Abortionists charged hundreds to thousands of dollars for abortions in the 1950s. Some women could not pay the fees or find abortionists, so they tried to self-induce a miscarriage using knitting needles, scissors, and crochet hooks. Those who could pay an abortionist often found themselves blindfolded and led to motel rooms where the illegal abortions were performed.

Abortion still sparks debate today, as many antiabortion activists work to ban abortion in the United States.

Programs, created during President Jimmy Carter's administration in 1978, was the first federal effort aimed at the issue. With its $60 million in funding, it provided health care, education, and social services to pregnant and parenting teens. This was equal to approximately $214 million in 2013.

In 1981, the Adolescent Family Life Act (AFLA) passed into law. It became known as the government's abstinence program. Its focus was teaching abstinence as the main preventative action for teen pregnancy. Opponents to the 1970 Family Planning federal program created this new program. AFLA proponents believed the Family Planning program promoted teen sexual activity and abortions.

This legislation highlights the battle of opinions in the United States concerning the best approach to teen pregnancy prevention. People question whether or not they should assume teens are having sex. If teens are having sex, many believe programs should focus on providing services and education to prevent pregnancies from happening. Some people wonder if the government should urge teens not to engage in sex. If so, perhaps prevention should focus on abstinence and the moral values of certain faiths or family groups. While this focus is still debated, the issue remains: 16 million teens give birth around the world each year, with approximately 368,000 of them in the United States.

CHAPTER
THREE

WHY DO TEENS GET PREGNANT?

The answer to why teens become pregnant seems obvious: they have sex. But there are several factors that can play into a teen pregnancy. Maybe the pregnancy happened after the girl missed one birth control pill. Perhaps the teens never learned about birth control but were curious about sex. Maybe the pregnancy was a result of rape. Other times, pregnancy is a goal for teens who believe they are ready to become parents.

For some teens, having a child seems to be an answer to the love absent from their own lives. They may have absent fathers or live in foster care. They may not get along with their parents or be neglected. They may want to have a baby because they believe a child could give them all the love they need. Most often, teens just do not realize a pregnancy could happen to them. They skip a birth control pill or choose not to use a condom

Some teen couples plan a pregnancy in hopes it will help or fix their relationship.

on one occasion. That one time could be all it takes. Teen pregnancy has many causes—both accidental and intentional. However the pregnancy happens, it is sure to alter the teens' lives.

Sexual Curiosity

Sexual curiosity is a very normal part of being a human. When puberty hits, teens have natural sexual urges due to their changing bodies and hormones. Differing societal views on teenage sex determine the kind of sexual education offered to teens. If a society

THE UNITED STATES VERSUS THE NETHERLANDS

Compared to the United States, the Netherlands has a very low teen pregnancy rate. In 2006, the US teen pregnancy rate was four times greater than the Netherland's rate. The Netherlands had 14.1 pregnancies for every 1,000 women ages 15 to 19, while the United States had 61.2 pregnancies per 1,000 teen women. This rate may reflect societal attitudes toward teen sex. In the United States, teen sex is discouraged and viewed negatively by adults. In the Netherlands, teen sex is generally accepted. According to the Advocates for Youth, teens in the Netherlands are more likely to use contraceptives than US teens. In a 2005 and 2007 study, 55 percent of teens in the Netherlands used the birth control pill, compared to only 11 percent of 15-year-old girls in the United States.[1]

Birth control pills can be ineffective if not taken every day as prescribed.

views teen sex negatively, it may direct education at remaining abstinent. If teen sex is more acceptable in a society, education may focus more on contraceptive use in an effort to prevent disease and pregnancy. Teens who receive abstinence-only education may not be aware of how to prevent pregnancy or have access to contraceptives. Some people believe this kind of education may contribute to teenage pregnancies. In some societies, where education focuses on teen sexuality and sex education, teen pregnancy rates have dropped.

Even if teens learn about birth control, they may not have easy access to it or understand how to properly use it. Many older US teens use contraception the first time they have sex, while teens who have sex at younger ages tend not to use contraception.

While birth control helps reduce the chance of becoming pregnant, it does not entirely eliminate

STATE-BY-STATE ACCESS

In the United States, minors have access to contraceptives in all states. But not all states allow the same type of access. Here is the breakdown of access for minors in different states:

- 21 states and the District of Columbia allow all minors access to contraceptive services. These include medical examinations and access to prescriptions.

- 4 states have no policies concerning minor access to contraceptives.

- 25 states have certain restrictions on minor access to contraceptive services. They include:

- Allowing access to minors if a doctor believes the minor would suffer health hazards without contraceptives

- Allowing access to married minors

- Allowing access to a minor who is a parent

- Allowing access to a minor who is or has been pregnant

- Allowing access to minors who are high school graduates, have reached a minimum age (which varies by state from 12 to 16), have demonstrated maturity, or have been referred by a certain professional, such as a physician or a clergy member.

the possibility. According to the Centers for Disease Control and Prevention (CDC), birth control pills have approximately a 9 percent failure rate, and condoms have an 18 percent failure rate.[2] Birth control pills often fail because the user forgets to take one every day. A 2012 study by the *New England Journal of Medicine* found unplanned pregnancies were 20 times more likely with women using the pill, patch, or vaginal ring versus women using an intrauterine device (IUD).[3] An IUD is inserted into the uterus to prevent pregnancy. Even with birth control, teens can become pregnant if they are sexually active. They are also at risk of contracting STDs.

A Need for Love

Sometimes teens want to get pregnant. They believe having a baby will fill an emotional need in their lives. For example, people often perceive babies as perfect and beautiful. Teens struggling with issues of low self-esteem may believe creating a perfect child will prove they can be successful. Many factors can cause emotional needs. Teens who have a need for love often have absent fathers. These teens may have single mothers who have limited time to spend with their children because they have to work long hours to pay for their living costs. They may have no parents to care for them and may be a part of the foster care system. Or they may be in a relationship that is not working well and believe a baby will make their partner stay with them.

Some teen parents may play the role of caretaker in their families, caring for their younger siblings. Once the younger siblings grow up and become independent, the teen loses the role of caretaker, creating a void some teens feel could be filled by becoming parents themselves.

Father absence is a large contributing factor to teenage pregnancy. Many studies show father absenteeism elevates the risk for early sexual activity and pregnancy in teen girls. Factors associated with father absenteeism also alter the courses of teens' lives. Families with absent fathers may live in poverty, have bad family relationships, or have a lack of parental control.

In a 2003 study, researchers in the United States and New Zealand observed groups of girls from age five until they reached 18. In both countries, the results showed the earlier the father was absent from a girl's life, the higher her pregnancy rate. In the United States, slightly

Studies have shown father involvement decreases the risk of teen pregnancy.

more than 30 percent of the girls with early absent fathers became pregnant, compared to approximately 6 percent of the girls with present fathers. In New Zealand, there was a similar result. Approximately 15 percent of girls whose fathers were absent carly in their lives became pregnant, compared to 4 percent of the girls with present fathers.[4]

Youth in foster care are also at a higher risk of becoming pregnant. In 2011, there were approximately 160,000 teens in foster care. Females in foster care or who have recently aged out of the foster care system are 2.5 times more likely to become pregnant by age 19 than females not in the system.[5] Foster care is often the result of abuse or neglect. It is difficult for teens to cope with these issues. Once in the system, teens are confronted with a whole new set of issues—a lack of stable relationships with adults, low self-esteem, and a strong need for love are just a few. While the government aims to provide a safe alternative to life in an abusive or neglected home, it can never replace the support offered by a family. Being in the foster care system can increase a child's risk of suffering from health or emotional problems. Children in the system may miss out on sex education due to changing

"Some young females actually want babies. It's not an accident because they feel like they want somebody that's going to love them. They don't have nobody."[6]
—Foster care youth from Georgia, interviewed for a study by the Georgia Campaign for Adolescent Power & Potential

foster placements and missing school. The sex education they do receive may come too late.

Sexual Violence

Sex may not be a choice for some teens. Some are raped, which can result in pregnancy. Adults sometimes seek out teens. Or teens may even be raped by one of their peers. When sexual violence is involved, it is highly likely contraception was not used, putting girls at risk of pregnancy and STDs.

A 2004 study for the *Journal of the American Academy of Pediatrics* linked sexual violence with high teen pregnancy rates. This study found girls who had experienced dating violence within the year before the study were twice as likely to become pregnant than girls who had not experienced violence.[7]

ETHNICITY AND TEEN PREGNANCY

On average, approximately 30 percent of US teens become pregnant before age 20. However, this rate is not the same for all ethnic groups. African American and Latina girls are much more likely to become pregnant than other ethnicities. According to the National Campaign to Prevent Teen and Unplanned Pregnancy, 50 percent of African American and 52 percent of Latina girls will become pregnant by age 20.[8]

Peer Pressure

For many teens, peer pressure affects their decision to have sex and use protection. In a 2012 survey of twelfth-grade girls, nearly 79 percent said there was pressure to be sexually experienced in high school.[9] Both boys and girls feel this pressure from peers. According to the National Campaign to Prevent Teen and Unplanned Pregnancy, 82 percent of boys ages 12 to 19 feel pressure to have sex, with most of this pressure coming from their friends.[10]

Sexual pressure can come from friends or partners in relationships. It can come through face-to-face interactions and also through digital interactions. Sexting—sending sexual images or text messages—is a common form of peer pressure. Some teens feel pressure to have more physical contact with the person he or she is texting after these kinds of sexual messages are exchanged. In a 2008 survey, 29 percent of teens ages 15 to 19 believed sexting between two people meant they were expected to date or have a sexual relationship.[11]

Another influence in making decisions about sex and protection is the use of drugs and alcohol. While under the influence, teens' judgment can be clouded. Teens

Sexting can be a gateway to physical contact for teens who feel pressured after sending sexual messages.

may put themselves in risky situations involving sex or violence. They often forget to use contraception, making themselves susceptible to STDs or pregnancy.

Teens make the choice to have unprotected sex for many reasons. However, teens who have been raped had no choice at all. If the result is pregnancy, the teen will have many difficult choices to make.

CHAPTER
FOUR

TOUGH CHOICES

A teenage pregnancy is often surprising. Teens who learn they are pregnant need to make difficult choices quickly. Should they abort the fetus? Should they keep the baby? Or, should they give up the baby for adoption? Each choice comes with its own set of realities. Teen parenthood can be a struggle, but adoption can be heartbreaking for the birth parents. Abortion may be the right choice for some, but for others, it goes against their morals or religious beliefs. Pregnancy progresses fairly quickly, and most abortions cannot be performed after the first three months. This means teens need to choose right away if they want to abort the fetus. Decisions such as these place a great deal of pressure on young, pregnant teens, but they have to make these choices. The first step to making the best decisions is becoming informed about their options. Teen clinics may be the first place teens turn to for pregnancy information.

Most often, teen pregnancies are not planned, leaving the unprepared teens to make quick decisions.

Many teens turn to Planned Parenthood, a clinic offering health exams, testing, treatment, and birth control services.

Teen Clinics

Many states offer free or low-cost sexual health-care clinics for teens. They provide contraceptives, pregnancy tests, and counseling to teens. They also screen for STDs. These clinics educate teens about the importance of prenatal care and provide referrals to doctors. They can also explain the options available regarding each teen's pregnancy. Many teens do not want to tell others they are pregnant. Teen clinics are a confidential source of information and help for teens in need of guidance and medical care.

Crisis Pregnancy Centers

Some clinics work to steer teens away from abortion and toward parenthood or adoption. These kinds of clinics are called crisis pregnancy centers. They may appear to be health-care clinics, but they are not. The people who run these centers are antiabortion. They can provide incorrect information. They may tell teens they can get breast cancer from an abortion. Or they may show movies or photos of abortions and aborted fetuses to patients to discourage them from choosing abortion.

Abortion

The Office of Adolescent Health reported 26 percent of US teen pregnancies ended in abortion in 2008.[1] Within the first three months of a pregnancy, abortion is an option. Doctors use a medical vacuum or other tool to remove the fetus from the uterus, ending the pregnancy. Abortion can be painful, and heavy bleeding is a possible risk. The in-clinic procedure costs $300 to $1,700. Some states require teens under the age of 18 to notify their parents before they can have an abortion. The abortion pill, RU-486, causes a woman to have a miscarriage within five hours to a few days of taking it.

Different issues arise with the choice of abortion. Adolescent boys do not have a legal say in the girl's decision to abort the fetus. So even if the boy wants to have the baby, the girl makes the final decision. Another issue relates to personal or religious beliefs. Although abortion is legal in the United States, people have differing thoughts about whether or not abortion is morally right. Sometimes protesters who believe abortion is wrong harass patients and doctors or keep them from entering abortion clinics. Abortion is a final decision and cannot be reversed. Coming to such a

HIDDEN PREGNANCIES

Facing the truth about a pregnancy can be too much to handle. Some teens feel unable to tell anyone they are pregnant. They hide their pregnancies by wearing baggy clothes and making excuses about their weight or morning sickness. Sometimes teens manage to keep their pregnancies secret for the full term, only revealing they are pregnant after the birth of their babies. Some deny the reality of their pregnancies. They cannot believe it is really happening and avoid dealing with it.

The denial sometimes continues after birth and can end in tragedy. In 2012, 14-year-old Florida teen Cassidy Goodson hid her pregnancy and gave birth to her son in her bathroom. She strangled her baby and put him in a shoe box, hiding the box in her room. The girl went to the hospital later that day to be treated for a miscarriage, which is what she told the nurses had occurred. But the medical staff realized the girl had delivered a baby and alerted police. The teen's mother found the baby's body three days later. Cassidy was charged with murder and sentenced to 18 months in a juvenile detention facility.

decision can be very difficult for confused and frightened pregnant teens.

Parenthood

Many teens decide to have their babies and become parents. Some make the choice to become pregnant, while others do not. Parenthood is difficult, even for adults who have planned for the changes a child brings. Having a child is costly and demanding, requiring many lifestyle changes. Some teens may have to quit school or find jobs to support their new families. Having a baby brings up many difficult questions and decisions. For most teens, it can be an overwhelming challenge whether or not they feel prepared.

Often, having a child means the teen mother will be a single parent. In a 2010 study, 88 percent of US teen mothers were unmarried when they gave birth.[2]

EMERGENCY CONTRACEPTIVES

Another way to halt a pregnancy is to take an emergency contraceptive pill, sometimes called the morning-after pill. These pills release hormones that can stop eggs from being released into the uterus or interfere with egg fertilization. It can be taken up to five days after having unprotected sex. One brand of the morning-after pill, Plan B, is available to men and women of any age without a prescription. Other emergency contraceptive pills are available with a prescription for teens under age 17. This is different from the abortion pill, RU-486.

Some teen couples live with their partners in unmarried relationships, while the majority of teens are single. Many teen mothers live with their parents or other adult relatives. According to the National Campaign to Prevent Teen and Unplanned Pregnancy, 72 percent of teen mothers lived with relatives or parents after the birth of their children in 2012.[3]

Along with making decisions about pregnancy, some couples also face the decision of marriage. While teen marriages were once common, they have become more rare in recent decades. In the late 1950s, the average US marriage age was 19. In 2013, the average age for a first marriage in the United States was 27 for women and 28.9 for men. Many teenage marriages fail. A 2001 CDC study showed teen marriages are two to three times more likely to end in divorce within ten years than the marriages of adults 25 years or older.[4] Sociologists believe teenage marriage failure happens because teens do not yet understand what they want in a lifetime partner. As they

"[Teens] may not know quite what they want in a lifetime partner. They still often have years of education to complete, as well as getting settled in the work world, and those two things may change their outlook on life considerably."[5]
—David Popenoe, codirector of the National Marriage Project at Rutgers University

grow older, wives and husbands may want different characteristics in a partner than they wanted as teens.

Although difficult, some young marriages do work, and getting married can be a better choice than single parenthood for teens. Older teens may be ready for the responsibilities of marriage. Many have other social responsibilities they already face, such as serving in the military and helping support their families by working. For teens who are ready, marriage may be the right choice for both themselves and the child.

Adoption

Some teens feel they are not ready to become parents but do not believe in abortion. Adoption may be the right choice for them. When choosing to put their babies up for adoption, teen mothers must carry their babies to full term, deliver their babies, and then sign over their rights as mothers to the new parents. Adoption can give the baby a life with more comfort and care than the teen parents could provide. At the same time, it can haunt the teen parents and the adopted child for their entire lives.

For teens choosing adoption, there are three types in the United States—open, semiopen, or closed. Each type has benefits and risks that need to be weighed carefully before making a decision. In the past, most adoptions were closed, meaning the adoption details were confidential. In a closed adoption, the birth parents and adoptive family do not meet each other. Once adopted, the birth parents cannot be involved in the adopted child's life. In an open adoption, the birth parents and adoptive parents meet or speak before the birth. They may continue to communicate throughout the child's life. The birth parents may also visit the child and his or her adoptive family. In some states, such as

JUNO

The 2007 movie *Juno* starring Ellen Page is about a pregnant teen who decides to give up her baby for adoption. The plan seems to work out perfectly for the pregnant teen—her baby gets a good home, and she finds a loving relationship with her baby's father. While many people enjoy the movie, some wonder if it glorifies teen pregnancy. It shows an ideal, yet often unrealistic, situation for the majority of teen moms. Most teens become single parents, while only approximately 2 percent give up their babies for adoption. Sarah Brown, CEO of the National Campaign to Prevent Teen and Unplanned Pregnancy, commented, "Adults understand the bigger picture and what the risks are of adolescence and childbearing. Adolescents see it through the lens of the 'me generation.' Adolescence is also a self-absorbed time. If the baby got handed off and she got the boyfriend back (as happens in *Juno*), what's the problem?"[6]

New York, once an open adoption is finalized, the child is legally regarded as the biological child of the adopting family. This means the adopting family may choose to cut off communication with the birth mother.

A semiopen adoption is a mixture of both open and closed adoptions. Birth and adoptive parents may share basic details about each other and communicate with the child through a third party, such as an adoption agency.

Adoptees and their birth parents often have many questions about each other. It is common for adoptees and their birth parents to seek out one another years after the adoption. This can, at times, be a rewarding search, but if one party does not want to make contact, it can be a painful and difficult experience.

Deciding whether or not to keep a child is a difficult decision for most teens. No matter their decision, life after the pregnancy will be different for them. Teen dads and moms must live with the reality of the choices they make. These choices affect their lives and also society as a whole.

CHAPTER
FIVE

TEEN MOMS

Parenting is never easy—especially for teens. It is difficult to imagine the sacrifice, time, and money required to raise a child. Teen moms must quickly adjust to life with a helpless infant. A child needs constant care, yet a teen mom must also think about the future. How will she finish school? How will she pay for the items her child needs? And sometimes moms or their babies have health issues related to their pregnancies or unprotected sex. In 2012, more than 300,000 babies were born to teen moms in the United States. Eighty-nine percent of the girls were not married.[1] Without a spouse or education, raising a child can be a difficult task.

Different Views

After learning they are pregnant, teen moms may be in denial or feel guilt and anger. News of their pregnancy can become a crisis for the teen mothers and their families. Parents of the teens may become angry or feel as if they have failed as parents, causing the teen

Many teen moms are unprepared for the realities of parenthood.

mother to feel guilt and shame. Fathers of the babies may be supportive, but others may completely abandon the mothers. Teachers, friends, and even strangers may give teen moms disapproving looks or say discouraging comments. Many stereotypes surround teenage pregnancy and parenthood. Some people think the mother is promiscuous. Others think teen mothers have ruined their lives. Teen moms may find they have few

A TEEN MOM'S LIFE

For 16-year-old teen mom Jennifer Reichert, a typical day starts at 5:00 a.m. Before leaving for school, she gets her 11-month-old daughter, Jamecia, ready for the day. Jennifer feeds Jamecia, puts baby lotion on her, dresses her, and packs her diaper bag. Jennifer gets herself ready and then walks to the bus stop with her daughter. The mother and daughter take the 15-minute bus ride to a special high school with a day care center: Croom's Academy in Florida. Jennifer gets to be near her daughter all day and still go to school. During the school day, Jennifer stops into the day care to feed her daughter or rock her to sleep. She also takes Jamecia to the school's clinic for a checkup and attends a parenting class at the school.

When school is done for the day, Jennifer still has many tasks and activities. She either goes to her part-time job at McDonald's or stays home and cares for her daughter. Both jobs are demanding, and Jennifer has little to no time to hang out with friends or study. Jamecia's father is involved, but he does not live in Florida. Jennifer's life revolves around her baby. She said, "There's no way you can put them on your schedule. You've got to be on theirs. A lot of times, you just want to quit." Despite the challenges raising her daughter, Jennifer says, "I wouldn't trade her for anything."[2]

people they can rely on for help with their pregnancies and babies.

Some teen mothers are kicked out of their homes by angry parents. The parents disapprove of their teen's actions and do not want to or cannot support another person in their household. This leaves the pregnant teen with no support and no place to live.

Other teens are already living on the streets when they become pregnant. Teen pregnancy rates are higher for homeless youth compared to housed youth. Some homeless teens use "survival sex"—trading sex for food or other needs—and become pregnant as a result. Others are raped. According to the National Network for Youth, 50 percent of homeless teens become pregnant compared to 33 percent of teens in homeless shelters and 10 percent of teens in permanent homes.[3]

For teen moms who need assistance, support groups, teen clinics, family centers, and group homes or shelters can help. These places can provide a sense of community and practical advice without judgment or shame. They can also help ensure teen moms and their babies have adequate housing, medical care, and food.

Health Effects

A teen pregnancy can have lasting health effects for teen moms. Prenatal care is important for both the mother and baby's health during the pregnancy, but teen moms are less likely to receive this care. If complications arise during a pregnancy, prenatal health visits can help identify them. One dangerous complication is preeclampsia, a condition that can develop after the twentieth week of pregnancy and cause a sudden rise in blood pressure. If untreated, it can be life threatening

THE PREGNANCY PROJECT

Washington state high school student Gaby Rodriguez tested the stereotypes of teen pregnancy in 2010 and 2011. As part of her social experiment, Gaby wore a fake pregnancy bulge under her clothing for 6.5 months. She told everyone she encountered she was pregnant. Only her mother, boyfriend, principal, and a few others knew the truth. Gaby fooled everyone. Her boyfriend's family, her siblings, friends, and teachers all believed she was pregnant. Gaby wanted to see how people would react to her pregnancy and if their perceptions of her would change because of it. She discovered perceptions did change, and rumors quickly spread. She said, "A lot of rumors were just that I was irresponsible. No college . . . it was bound to happen. I knew she would get pregnant. Doesn't she know she just ruined her life."[4] Gaby revealed her experiment to the school during an assembly. She later published a book about the experience and her findings called The Pregnancy Project, which was made into a movie for the cable network Lifetime.

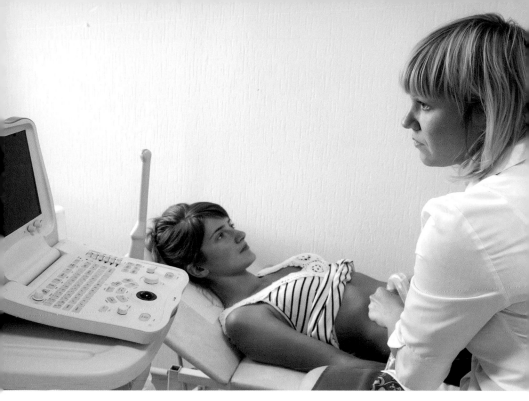

Many teen mothers are unaware of the importance of prenatal care or are unable to afford it.

for both the mother and baby. Preeclampsia is more likely to happen to teens. The younger the teen, the higher the risk for this complication. One 2010 study found teen mothers under the age of 15 were twice as likely to develop preeclampsia as mothers aged 15 to 18.[5] The only cure for preeclampsia is to deliver the baby, which can be very premature. Young mothers are also at risk of developing anemia, and their children can have low birth weights or be stillborn.

STDs, such as chlamydia and gonorrhea, may affect the health of teen moms. According to a 2004 study, people ages 15 to 24 made up approximately 50 percent of all new STD cases of the entire sexually active population.[6] Chlamydia is the most commonly contracted STD for teens ages 15 to 19. If untreated, chlamydia can make women infertile. Gonorrhea and genital human papillomavirus (HPV) are two other STDs common in this age group.

Education

Going to school can be difficult or nearly impossible for the mother of a newborn. A newborn needs constant care—from frequent diaper changes to scheduled feedings. Many teen moms lack access to day care and must stay home with their babies. This forces them to quit school or postpone graduation. Their education suffers, and many teen moms fall behind their nonparenting peers. This educational setback can affect their lives for years, keeping teen moms from achieving well-paying jobs and decent standards of living. Many teen moms and their children live in poverty as a result. This poverty is often difficult to break, continuing across generations as a result.

Teen moms are 10 to 12 percent less likely to complete high school and 14 to 29 percent less likely to attend college than mothers who wait to have children until age 30 or older.[7] Overall, teen moms have approximately two fewer years of education than older moms. According to a 2008 report, nearly 50 percent of teen moms do not graduate from high school and 30 percent do not get a GED.[8] But there are several choices for teen moms who want to continue their education. Some alternative schools offer in-school day care for teen moms, and there are online school programs and GED options for parenting teens.

Providing for the Baby

With less education, teen moms become less employable. Many live in poverty or have very low earnings. Some teen moms average just $6,500 per year for their first 15 years as parents. Many teen moms

Teen parents often work minimum-wage paying jobs in an effort to provide for their child.

are single parents who rely on public assistance for nearly the first five years as parents. They also utilize food stamps, public housing (government-supported housing for people with low incomes), and medical assistance funds. According to the National Campaign to Prevent Teen and Unplanned Pregnancy, approximately 25 percent of teen moms are on welfare.[9] These government payments are available to teen moms who are unable to support themselves within three years of their child's birth.

Teen moms may or may not receive child support from the teen fathers if they are single parents. A father is required to support his child but may neglect this responsibility and not pay support. If a father does pay child support, the amount he pays is based on his income, which is often very low. A teen father pays an average of $800 for child support each year.

Another factor affecting the poverty levels of teen moms is the birth of a second child. Approximately 25 percent of teen moms have a second child within 24 months of the birth of their first child.[10] A second child can make it even more difficult for teen moms to find jobs or complete their education. Teen moms are not the only ones affected by the birth of a child. Teen dads have to make major life changes as well.

A BABY'S COST

Children are expensive to raise. The United States Department of Agriculture regularly reports on the cost of raising children in the United States. It estimates the total cost from birth to age 18 for a single-parent family is $161,220 per child. In a two-parent household that number rises to $173,490.[11]

CHAPTER
SIX

TEEN DADS

For every pregnant teen mother, there is a father who is equally responsible for the new baby. Yet, people often forget about teen dads in the issue of teen pregnancy. There are many services for teen moms, but there are few services available to help teen dads. Some teen dads may not know what the role of a father is if they have grown up in single-parent families with absent fathers. Stereotypes surround teen fathers. Many people assume teen fathers will have little to no involvement in their child's future. For some that is true, but many teen dads want to be involved with their children and work hard to provide for them.

Teen dads face a number of issues when it comes to parenting their children. If they are not in relationships with the moms but still wish to be involved with their children, they must arrange shared custody for their child. They must find a way to support their child and aim for an economically stable future. Without support, teen dads can feel alone in this struggle.

While some fathers are older than the teen moms, approximately 30 to 50 percent of babies born to teen moms also have teen dads.

Different Views

Until the baby is born, a teen male does not have a say in the female's choices surrounding the pregnancy. A female may choose to end the pregnancy with an abortion even if the male wants to have the child. Teen females and their families can also cut off

A TEEN DAD'S LIFE

Single dad Travis Luciano had his son, TJ, at the age of 17. Two months after TJ was born, Travis and the mother split up. Travis later gained full custody of his son, which is uncommon for teen dads. Travis quit high school, got his GED, and as of 2010 worked at the Bronx Zoo in New York making $7.25 an hour.

Travis and his son shared a small, two-bedroom apartment with his mother and sister. His paychecks helped, but he did not earn enough money to provide for all of his son's needs. Elizabeth Porter, Travis's mom, paid for almost everything—from TJ's diapers and bottles to the bills.

When Travis got home from work, it was often late at night. Sometimes he was tired, but parenthood is a full-time job. He said, "Sometimes I get home from work and I'm extra tired because there were a million guests at the zoo one day, and I just wanna go to sleep and I get home and he's still up, and he still wants to play, and he hasn't seen daddy since this morning and he's running to me and I can't. I'm sorta used to it by now but there's just those days when you just need [a pill] for your headache cause you're doing this by yourself."[1] While life is not easy for teen dad Travis, he loves his son dearly—he just wishes he had waited a few more years to become a father.

communication with teen males. These situations can be very difficult and emotional for the males.

Teen fathers can be viewed as uncaring and irresponsible. Many assume the fathers will not be involved in their children's lives. While some fathers do become absent, others stay and want to be involved. A study by the Ford Foundation and the Bank Street College of Education followed nearly 400 teen dads in eight US cities. The study found 82 percent of the fathers had daily contact with their kids, and 74 percent of the fathers helped support them.[2] The earlier the fathers connected with their babies, the more likely it was they stayed in their children's lives.

Resources for Teen Dads

Teen pregnancy attention and research often focuses on teen mothers, so studies on teen fathers are lacking. Public resources are also often lacking. In the 2000s, teen fatherhood programs emerged, providing much needed resources to young fathers. Some of the best programs partner with prenatal clinics and programs for teen mothers. They also offer incentives to the dads, such as free diapers or condoms. Being involved with a program can be valuable to teen fathers who feel

Some programs for teen fathers offer small group sessions, providing a place to communicate with and confide in others dealing with the same situation.

isolated and afraid. They can gain a sense of community with other teen dads and learn important job and parenting skills.

Education

As is the case with teen mothers, many teen fathers do not complete high school or attend college. A 2011 study of male teens with partners who miscarried and partners who gave birth found teen fathers were 15 percent less likely to graduate from high school and more likely to get a GED.[3] Similar to teen moms, fathers who do not graduate from high school limit their work options later in life. With limited opportunities, they can enter a cycle of poverty and have difficulties paying child support and providing for their children.

Providing for the Baby

Father involvement is very important to the health and development of a child. But most

THE L.A. FATHER'S PROGRAM

To help teen dads ease into fatherhood, the L.A. Fathers Program in California provides relationship classes, parenting classes, job training, and other social services. It began in 2012 at the Children's Hospital Los Angeles, complimenting an established program for teen mothers. The teen fathers get together and discuss the challenges of parenting at a young age. Program coordinator Frank Blaney said, "A lot of young dads feel alienated and experience a lot of judgment—from their family, from their friends, at school. Here, there are other dads that are going through the same experience they are."[4] The program also stresses the importance of education to achieve long-term financial stability.

teen fathers do not live in the same home as their babies. According to a 2012 report, 44 percent of teen dads lived with their children from birth, meaning 56 percent did not.[5] Having a good relationship with the father can prevent future behavior problems. According to a 2006 study, boys and girls not involved with their fathers are twice as likely to abuse drugs or drop out of school.[6] Teen fathers who do not live with their children have to arrange shared custody or visitation times in order to see their children. A 2012 report from the National Campaign to Prevent Teen and Unplanned Pregnancy stated 50 percent of teen fathers had not visited their child in the past month. The remaining 50 percent had visited their child at least once or twice in the past month.[7]

Aside from emotional support, teen dads are required to provide financial support for their children. The same 2012 report found only 24 percent

ESTABLISHING PATERNITY

Maternity is self-evident during a pregnancy, but paternity is not as simple to determine. Teen dads can request a paternity test before legally acknowledging they fathered a child. A paternity test looks at the DNA of both the child and the father. If there is a match, the male knows he is definitely the father of the child. To establish paternity, the teen must legally acknowledge his biological child. Once he does, he is financially responsible for the child until the child turns 18 and is a legal adult.

Teen mothers and fathers often struggle to maintain civil relationships, especially when the father is not able to provide child support.

of teen mothers receive child support from the fathers.[8] With limited earning potential, teen dads often find it difficult to pay child support. The financial burden then falls to the mothers and often their extended families.

CHAPTER
SEVEN

CHILDREN OF TEENS

While many teen parents face emotional and financial difficulties, the children of teen parents are not automatically at a disadvantage. Every child grows up in unique circumstances. If the extended families of the teen parents are supportive, both emotionally and financially, the child will most likely have a very comfortable life. But if the teen parents do not receive financial support from their families, they can find themselves in poverty. Poverty can lead to some self-perpetuating effects for the children of teens.

Immaturity may also stunt the teens' parenting skills, putting their children at risk for abuse, neglect, or foster care. While not all children of teens suffer these negative results, research shows some trends in the issues they face throughout their lives and into adulthood. These issues have social and economic costs, as well as emotional and physical.

Children of teen parents are more likely to suffer from poverty and health-care issues than children born to adult parents.

A mother's health habits during pregnancy, such as smoking or eating poorly, affect the child's health.

Health and Cognitive Issues

A teen mom's level of prenatal care and age can affect the health of her baby. If there was little prenatal care, issues that could have been prevented may go unnoticed until the child is born. Babies born to teen mothers are more likely to have low birth weights or be born prematurely than babies born to mothers aged 20 to 39. These issues can lead to a number of health problems for the child, including blindness, cerebral palsy, chronic respiratory problems, or even death. According to a 2008 study, 20 percent of children born to teen mothers have long-term health problems.[1]

Research shows children of younger mothers are behind children born to mothers ages 20 or 21 in cognitive skills when starting kindergarten. They tend to have lower scores

LOW BIRTH WEIGHT

A baby's birth weight can indicate the likelihood of future health problems. A low birth weight is less than 5.5 pounds (2.5 kg). The causes of low birth weight include the age of the mother (younger than 15 or older than 35) and the mother's lifestyle habits. Habits capable of causing low birth weight include smoking, drinking alcohol, and eating poorly, resulting in a lack of necessary weight gain. During prenatal care, doctors can identify problems that may lead to a baby's low birth weight and advise the mother about how to prevent health problems for her baby.

Studies have shown children of teen mothers perform at lower levels in school compared to children of adult mothers.

on standardized tests and are 50 percent more likely to repeat a grade.[2] As the children grow older, they are more likely to drop out of high school. One study found only 66 percent of children born to young mothers graduated from high school on time, while 81 percent of children born to mothers aged 20 to 21 graduated on time.[3]

Children of teen parents are more likely to become the victims of abuse or neglect. Teens who do not have well-developed parenting skills may not see signs of sickness or other issues with their child. In addition, parenting is very stressful and teens may not be ready to deal with those emotions. They may take out their anger and stress on their children both verbally and physically. In an Illinois-based study, children of teen parents were twice as likely as children of mothers ages 20 to 21 to report they had been abused or neglected.[4] When the abuse or neglect of a child is reported, the child can be removed from the home and placed in foster care.

FOSTER CARE

Studies show teen mothers are likely to become more stressed from parenting than older mothers. This can result in dysfunctional parenting skills leading to abuse or neglect. According to the National Campaign to Prevent Teen and Unplanned Pregnancy, teen mothers ages 17 and younger are 2.2 times more likely to place a child in foster care than older mothers. They are also twice as likely to be reported for child abuse or neglect.[5]

Research also shows children in the foster care system are at a disadvantage compared to children who grow up with their families. Foster kids have more emotional and behavioral problems than their peers and have high rates of school suspensions and expulsions. A 2005 study of foster youth in Illinois, Wisconsin, and Iowa found more than 33 percent of foster children never graduate from high school or attain a GED. Foster youth are less employed than their peers as well. The same study found 40 percent of foster youth were employed compared to 60 percent of their peers who were not in the foster care system.[6]

Studies have proved there is an increase in served
jail time for sons born to teen mothers.

Future of the Children

Sons of teen parents are more at risk of being jailed. According to the National Campaign to Prevent Teen and Unplanned Pregnancy, sons of teen parents are 2.2 times more likely to serve time in jail than sons born to mothers aged 20 to 21. Fourteen percent of the sons of teen parents serve jail time by their late 30s, while only 6 percent of the sons born to older mothers served time.[7] Spending time in jail can affect the earning potential and educational achievements of these men. This can add to the likelihood of future poverty.

The daughters of teen parents may become teen mothers themselves. The National Campaign to Prevent Teen and Unplanned Pregnancy study found the risk is high—nearly 33 percent of the daughters of teen mothers became pregnant as teens.[8] If the child is placed in foster care, there is an added risk of

"Reducing teen pregnancy not only improves the well-being of children, youth, and families, it saves taxpayer dollars. At a time when policymakers and others are intensely focused on cost-saving measures, funding proven efforts to reduce teen pregnancy is important, timely, and should be a high priority."[9]
—Sarah Brown, CEO of the National Campaign to Prevent Teen and Unplanned Pregnancy

teen pregnancy. Young women in foster care are twice as likely to become pregnant by age 19 than their peers who are not in foster care.[10] These factors create or continue a pattern of teen childbearing and poverty that can stretch from one generation to the next.

Economic and Social Costs

Teen childbearing financially affects the lives of the teens and their children. It also affects general society. Taxpayer costs at the local, state, and federal levels are staggering. It is estimated teen childbearing cost US taxpayers $10.9 billion in 2008, which equals approximately $1,647 per teen mother. A large part of that estimate—$3.2 billion— is the lost tax revenue (fees taken from a person's income to support the government) of the children of teen parents, who may have less education and less earning potential. Teen childbearing also results in an estimated $2.3 billion in taxpayer costs for public health care, $2.8 billion for child

BIRTHRATES: STATE-BY-STATE

Teen birthrates vary from state to state in the United States. New Mexico had the highest teen birthrate in 2012, with 45.7 children born to every 1,000 teen girls aged 15 to 19. New Hampshire had the lowest teen birthrate in the country, with 13.8 children born to every 1,000 teen girls.[11]

welfare costs, and $2.3 billion in costs for incarceration of the grown children of teen parents.[12] These costs are not equal from state to state. Some states have much higher incidences of teen pregnancy and childbearing than others and some participate more in publicly funded programs.

Because of these high public costs, teen pregnancy and childbearing has become an important political issue in the United States. Billions of dollars are allocated each year to deal with the negative consequences of teen pregnancy. The issue remains a critical one in the United States, but it is also a global issue.

CHAPTER
EIGHT

A GLOBAL ISSUE

Most of the world's teen births happen in developing countries—approximately 95 percent.[1] A developing country is one that experiences high poverty levels. As in the United States, teen pregnancy and childbirth drastically change a woman's life in a developing country. Her education may stop, she may become dependent on others, and she may not be able to work. Many developing countries have male-dominated societies in which women have fewer rights and opportunities to succeed independently. An early pregnancy and child can further limit a young woman's opportunities and steer her toward a life of poverty.

Child Brides

Nine out of ten teen pregnancies in developing countries happen within marriage.[2] Many teen girls in developing countries are forced into early marriages by their parents. The expectation is for them to become

Young teen girls in developing countries are often pressured or forced into early marriages, resulting in early pregnancy.

pregnant and have children. Their risk for pregnancy-related health problems is high. They also have very limited access to education and information about contraceptives, as many leave school at such young ages.

According to the United Nations Population Fund (UNFPA), 140 million girls under the age of 18 will be married between 2011 and 2020 worldwide. Of those 140 million, 50 million will be under the age of 15. Child marriages happen to both boys and girls but at much higher rates for girls. Most of these marriages take place in parts of Africa and South Asia. In South Asia, nearly 50 percent of girls are married by age 18. In sub-Saharan African countries, nearly one-third of the girls marry by age 18.[3]

In developing countries, pressure to marry and have children comes from many levels—from government laws denying access to contraception to a husband's refusal to wear a condom. Schools may not teach sex

Despite a law banning child marriage, some Indian teens are still married off at young ages.

education, and families may leave their daughters with no choice but to marry the men chosen for them. Young brides are often girls from very poor families who have low levels of education and live in rural areas. Often, there are few opportunities for women, and the girls' families cannot afford to keep them in their households. Families may believe they are giving their daughters better lives by marrying them to older men. The families may see marriage as an escape from their family's poverty.

Violence and Abuse

Young girls in developing countries may be paired with much older men through arranged marriages. A UNFPA study found the greater the age difference between a husband and wife, the more likely the wife was to give birth before age 18.[5] These young girls tend to be more susceptible to sexual abuse and physical violence from their husbands.

According to the WHO and UNFPA, 150 million teen girls around the world have sex forced upon them, and many teens lose their virginity to forced sex each year. Strangers may force sex on the teens, or it may be husbands who force their wives to have sex. One survey of 14 countries found 64 percent of girls aged 15 to 24 in the Democratic

"I knew about condoms, but could not ask my husband to use one. I was only 16 when I got married and felt he would get angry, as I was less educated than him."[6]
—Pinki, 19, India

Republic of the Congo were forced into their first sexual experience.[7]

When the girl's husband is much older, it is even more difficult for the teen to convince her husband to use contraception, especially if she has left school early and has had little education. This puts girls at risk for pregnancy and STDs. Even while pregnant, young girls are at risk for physical abuse from their husbands. The WHO estimates one in five teen girls are physically abused during pregnancy.[8] This abuse puts both the mother and infant at risk for developing health problems.

Health Issues

If teens in developing countries become pregnant, several factors put them at risk of death or injury during pregnancy or childbirth. Many come from poverty and are malnourished, which can cause nutritional anemia. Having this condition can result in miscarriage, stillbirth, premature birth, and the mother's death. Young girls also have physically immature bodies. Their birth canals and pelvises are not ready for labor and childbirth. They may also have unsafe abortions.

Girls who have physically immature bodies are at risk of developing obstetric fistula. This condition results from a long labor in a body not fully developed. During labor, the baby's head tears the walls of the girl's rectum and bladder. After delivering the baby, the girl is unable to control her urine or feces. The condition can be

MERESO KILUSU

In Tanzania, child marriage among the Maasai tribe is common. At the age of 13, Mereso Kilusu was married to a man in his 70s. In her community, the men decide when a girl is to be married. Sometimes, marriages happen to form relationships between families. Other times, they are decided for financial reasons. The husband pays the girl's parents for the marriage. That is what happened to Kilusu, who eventually had five children with her husband and then escaped the marriage. She now speaks out against child marriage to the international community. She reflects on her marriage and having children at a young age:

I was married at 13 to a man in his 70s. It happened during Christmas break. My father told my school that I had died. Even if he hadn't, I would have been forced to leave when I got pregnant because that was the law at the time. I gave birth to my first child within a year. I had no professional prenatal care and no trained medical assistance during delivery. I had to depend on my husband and his other wives for guidance. It was a very painful experience. Every time I became pregnant after that I felt sick and scared. Because of all these difficult births I have a hard time controlling my bladder and it can be painful to urinate. Today, I am a mother of five at 29 years old.[9]

fixed through surgery, but it is not affordable or widely available in developing countries. Many young mothers must live with this problem and are often isolated from their communities and homes because of the condition. There are between 2 and 3.5 million girls in developing countries living with obstetric fistula.[10]

Unsafe abortions are a leading cause of pregnancy-related complications in developing countries. These abortions are performed by a person who is untrained or lacking medical skills. Abortion is illegal in many developing countries, where approximately 98 percent of the world's unsafe abortions are performed.[11] Adolescents are more likely than adults to experience complications from these abortions. The complications include hemorrhaging (the rapid and uncontrollable loss of blood), organ damage, sterility, or even death.

These childbirth and pregnancy-related complications are the leading causes of death for girls ages 15 to 19 in developing countries. The UNFPA estimates 70,000 teens in developing countries die each year due to these complications. Infants are also at a higher risk of death when born to adolescent mothers. Adolescent mothers are 50 percent more likely to have

Remaining in school is often not an option for teen
mothers in developing countries, where the mothers
are forced to work and care for their children.

stillbirths or newborns that die shortly after birth than mothers aged 20 to 29.[12]

Education and Contraception

Along with medical complications, teen moms in developing countries also face educational disadvantages. As in the United States, the teen mother's education is likely cut short. The longer she stays in school, the less likely a girl will become pregnant at a young age, but this is not an option for many teen girls in developing countries. Girls who leave school early may miss receiving sex and pregnancy prevention education offered in schools.

There may be other community factors blocking these young girls' access to contraceptive information and services. Some countries have laws stopping teens under age 18 from accessing contraceptive and sexual health services unless they have parental or spousal consent. Different social beliefs also determine the availability of contraceptives in different communities.

In certain African countries, people view childbearing as a woman's main value in society and believe contraception devalues a woman. Unmarried women have more difficulty accessing contraception in countries where premarital sex is considered immoral. In these places, people believe the woman should not be having sex in the first place. In countries where sons are highly valued, a husband may forbid his young wife from using contraception until she gives birth to a son. Husbands may beat their wives or divorce them if they fail to become pregnant, making wives afraid to use contraception.

While adolescent pregnancy in developing countries is a complex issue, measures are being taken to slow the birthrates of teens in some countries. Keeping girls in school longer helps deter marriage and pregnancy. In Kenya, providing free school uniforms keeps girls in school longer and helps reduce the pregnancy rate by 17 percent.[14] In Zimbabwe, a program aimed at reducing STDs unintentionally reduced teen pregnancy rates. Providing support networks to girls in underprivileged areas also helps them remain childless longer. In Guatemala, the *Abriendo Oportunidades* (Open Opportunities) project started girls' clubs for Mayan girls —a group that typically lives in poverty, has limited education, and bears children at a young age. The clubs helped more girls stay in school longer and delayed pregnancies. Through various initiatives in different countries, teens are receiving the support they need to stay in school, remain unmarried, and delay pregnancy.

Delaying childbirth allows women to achieve higher education and income levels. This helps reduce poverty and ensures better health for children. The children have better lives overall, and society benefits as well.

CHAPTER
NINE

TEEN PREGNANCY PREVENTION

Different societies see the negative effects teen pregnancy can have on its communities. While some teen pregnancies have positive outcomes, the ones that do not have some lasting consequences. For example, the effects of living in poverty can influence future teen pregnancies. This cycle of poverty and pregnancy can impose great financial costs to communities and taxpayers, in addition to the negative effects it has on the individual families.

Policymakers, educators, and researchers study teen pregnancy to determine how to lower its rates. Teen pregnancy prevention strategies are developed through studies, laws, and different programs. When implemented, they can help lower rates of teen pregnancies and their costs to society. No single program can eliminate teen pregnancy, but by using a

Poverty can begin with a teen pregnancy and continue across several generations.

> "I felt alone. So, I just was like, I think I could have a baby [and the baby] will love me back. So, then I wouldn't have to worry about someone else loving me. . . . I don't think a baby would hurt me the way other people have. . . . I definitely felt like I would have unconditional love for real.[1]
>
> —Sandie, 17-year-old pregnant teen

combination of methods, the message can reach a diverse population of young adults.

Meeting Emotional Needs

Teens who want babies usually have an emotional need that is not being met. They feel lonely and uncared for and believe a baby is the answer to their emotional needs. A baby will love them unconditionally and will always be there for them. These teens are not looking very far into the future. They see the love a baby could offer but do not see the practical needs of a baby or understand the challenges in meeting those needs.

How can these teens fill their emotional needs? It starts at home with parents. Parental involvement is critical in the prevention of teen pregnancy. Ideally, this involvement includes both parents, as research shows families with absent fathers have higher incidences of teen pregnancy. Families with parents who have close relationships with their children, are involved with their children's activities, and who live in the same home as their children have lower incidences of early teen sex and pregnancy. Teens value the advice their parents have to offer as well. In a 2012 survey of US parents and teens, both boys and girls ages 12 to 19 said parents have the most influence on their decisions about sex.[2]

Parents need to have open communication with their teens about sex, their moral beliefs about premarital sex, and the use of contraception. Many parents do not know their teens are having sex. Most want to know, though, so they can talk with their teens about using contraception to avoid pregnancy. In the same 2012 survey of US parents and teens, 79 percent of the parents wanted to know if their teen was having sex, 9 percent said they would be angry to know, 4 percent said they would rather not know, and 8 percent did not know how they felt about the issue.[3] Talking about sex with a child can be very uncomfortable and difficult, but open communication about contraception has a positive effect. Teens who talk with their parents are more likely to be consistent with their use of contraception.

Sex Education

Teen pregnancy is declining in the United States, yet the country still has one of the highest teen pregnancy rates of all developed countries. This makes sex education an extremely important and also controversial issue. Education and services are provided to make teens aware of the issue of teen pregnancy and what can be done to prevent it.

In the United States, sex education has historically fallen into two main categories: abstinence-only education and comprehensive sex education. Abstinence-only education focuses on refraining from sex to prevent teen pregnancy and STDs. Contraceptives are mentioned minimally if at all. Advocates of this type of sex education argue abstinence is the only 100 percent effective method of preventing disease and unplanned pregnancies. The abstinence-only method works only if teens refrain from sex. This type of education was the most used and highly funded in the United States from 1996 to 2009.

Comprehensive sex education includes information about abstinence and its benefits, but it also teaches youth about condoms and contraception to prevent pregnancy and STDs. Youth also learn about communication and relationship skills and the importance of defining values and goals to help guide their decisions about having sex. In 2010, the US government began funding comprehensive sex education programs.

VIRGINITY PLEDGES

Abstinence-only education promotes virginity pledges to teens. A virginity pledge is a vow a teen makes to wait until marriage to have sex. An evangelical Christian group first presented this idea in 1993. Millions of teens have taken the pledge in the United States. Some argue the pledges are meaningless, while others say they help teens abstain from sex longer than their peers.

A 2008 study looked at both pledge takers and nontakers. Five years after taking the pledge, researchers found both groups had similar levels of premarital sex. The pledge takers did wait longer to have sex, until approximately 21 years old compared with age 17 for the nontakers. The study also found pledge takers were less likely to use birth control than those who did not take the pledge.

The study's researcher, Janet Rosenbaum, PhD, said, "Virginity pledgers are very different than most US teens—they are obviously more conservative, they have more negative views about sexuality and birth control and so, even if they didn't take a pledge, these would be teenagers who would be very likely to abstain anyhow."[5]

Government Funding

In 2013, the US federal government funded several programs aimed at preventing teen pregnancy. The Teen Pregnancy Prevention (TPP) program received $105 million to provide grants for programs and research. The programs include curriculum to teach youth about pregnancy prevention, relationships, and responsible behavior. They also focus on youth development, such as arts or sports groups, aimed at helping teens avoid risky behaviors.

The Personal Responsibility Education Program (PREP) receives $75 million each year to fund programs educating youth about abstinence and contraception. The money must be used for programs following effective models chosen by the US Department of Health and Human Services. These programs must also include adult preparation classes, such as financial literacy education, career success, and healthy life skills.

Title V Abstinence Education receives $50 million per year. This money funds programs teaching youth only about the values of abstinence before marriage and the harmful effects of sex before marriage.

Staci Williams speaks to ninth grade students about safe sex practices and STD awareness as part of the Teen Pregnancy Prevention Collaborative in Detroit, Michigan, in 2010.

Programs receiving these grants may not teach youth about contraception.

Both the TPP and PREP programs are modeled after other programs that have had proven results in teen pregnancy prevention. With a more diverse approach, these programs may reach a larger number of teens. The hope is to reduce the US teen pregnancy rate. There is no one solution to preventing teen pregnancy, but with more education, teens can make informed choices about their futures.

TIMELINE

1880
Abortion is illegal in all US states.

1950s
It is common for US teens to marry
and become pregnant.

1960
The US government approves use of the birth control pill.

1970
The US government creates the Family Planning
federal program.

1972
Title IX of the Education Amendments Act bans
public schools from expelling pregnant teens.

1972
Girls 18 years and older no longer need parental
permission to get a prescription for the birth control pill.

1973

The US Supreme Court decision in the *Roe v. Wade* case rules women in all states have the right to an abortion if they want one during their first trimester.

1978

The US government creates the Office of Adolescent Pregnancy Programs, the first federal effort aimed at teen pregnancy.

1981

The Adolescent Family Life Act passes into law. It becomes known as the government's abstinence program, focusing on teaching abstinence as the main preventative action for teen pregnancy.

1996–2009

The US government heavily funds abstinence-only education.

2006

The US teen pregnancy rate is four times that of the Netherland's rate.

2007

The movie *Juno* about a pregnant teen who decides to give up her baby for adoption opens in theaters.

TIMELINE

2008
Estimates report teen pregnancy costs US taxpayers $10.9 billion for the year.

2008
Twenty-six percent of US teen pregnancies end in abortion.

2010
Teens have 367,752 babies in the United States.

2010
The US government begins funding comprehensive sex education programs.

2010–2011
Teen Gaby Rodriguez fakes a pregnancy at her high school as a social experiment in stereotypes against teen moms.

2011–2020
The United Nations Population Fund
estimates 140 million girls under age 18
will be married around the world.

2012
Florida teen Cassidy Goodson delivers and
kills her son after hiding her pregnancy.

2012
Teen dads turn to the newly formed L.A.
Father's Program to support their needs.

2013
The average age for a first marriage in the United
States is 27 for women and 28.9 for men.

2013
Forty-four states have laws requiring teens
to have consent from a parent or to notify a
parent in order to have an abortion.

ESSENTIAL FACTS

At Issue

- The United States has one of the highest teen pregnancy rates of all developed countries in the world.

- Young mothers and fathers drop out of high school to care for their children and get jobs. Without an education, the young parents must often take low-paying jobs. This leads to poverty, which can extend into the adult lives of their children.

- The children of teen parents are likely to enter the foster care system due to abuse or neglect. Once in the foster care system, children can suffer emotional and developmental issues. Teen girls in the foster care system are also more likely to become pregnant.

- Teen fathers lack programs to support their needs. Most teen pregnancy programs focus on the needs of teen mothers.

- Sex education in the United States was once mainly focused on abstinence-only programs. It now includes a combination of abstinence and contraception education.

- Teen pregnancy is a global issue. Many girls in developing countries are forced to become child brides and bear children at young ages. Many develop serious health problems from their pregnancies and are forced to leave school.

Critical Dates

1972

Title IX of the Education Amendments Act bans public schools from expelling pregnant teens. This means teen mothers may still attend school throughout their pregnancies.

1973

The US Supreme Court decision in the *Roe v. Wade* case rules women in all states have the right to an abortion if they want one during their first trimester.

2010

The US government begins funding comprehensive sex education programs. This education teaches both abstinence and contraceptive use.

Quote

"Reducing teen pregnancy not only improves the well-being of children, youth, and families, it saves taxpayer dollars. At a time when policymakers and others are intensely focused on cost-saving measures, funding proven efforts to reduce teen pregnancy is important, timely, and should be a high priority." —*Sarah Brown, CEO of the National Campaign to Prevent Teen and Unplanned Pregnancy*

GLOSSARY

abortion
The induced ending of a pregnancy through a medical procedure during the first 12 weeks of the pregnancy.

absenteeism
The tendency to be away.

abstinence
The act of refraining from sexual intercourse.

anemia
A condition in which a person's body produces fewer red blood cells, causing the person to feel very tired and weak.

child support
Payments made by a parent to support a child living in the other parent's home.

contraception
A drug, device, or method used to deliberately prevent pregnancy.

custody
The care of a child by a guardian.

fetus
A developing human from two months after conception to its birth.

foster care
A program providing care for orphaned, neglected, or abused children.

morals
Principals or rules of conduct by which a person lives.

paternity
The state of being a father.

poverty
The state of a person who lacks the necessary amount of money or possessions to live comfortably.

prenatal
Occurring before the birth of a child.

promiscuous
Not limited to one sexual partner.

rape
To force an unwilling person to have sex by means of violence or threats.

sexually transmitted disease
A disease spread through sexual intercourse.

stereotype
A widely held but simple idea, opinion, or image of a person or group.

stigma
A mark of shame or discredit.

stillbirth
The birth of a dead fetus.

ADDITIONAL RESOURCES

Selected Bibliography

"Adolescent Pregnancy." *World Health Organization*. WHO, 2012. Web. 28 Nov. 2013.

Hoffman, Saul D., and Rebecca Maynard, eds. *Kids Having Kids: Economic Costs and Social Consequences of Teen Pregnancy*. Washington DC: Urban Institute, 2008. Print.

Stewart Ng, Alison, and Kelleen Kaye. "Teen Childbearing, Single Parenthood, and Father Involvement." *The National Campaign to Prevent Teen and Unplanned Pregnancy*. The National Campaign to Prevent Teen and Unplanned Pregnancy, Oct. 2012. Web. 27 Nov. 2013.

Williamson, Nancy. "Motherhood in Childhood: Facing the Challenge of Adolescent Pregnancy." *Save the Children*. Save the Children, 2013. Web. 27 Nov. 2013.

Further Readings

Alters, Sandra. *Abortion: An Eternal Social and Moral Issue*. Farmington Hills, MI: Gale Cengage, 2012.

Krueger, Lisa, ed. *Teen Pregnancy and Parenting*. Farmington Hills, MI: Gale Cengage, 2011. Print.

Sheen, Barbara. *How Can Teen Pregnancy Be Reduced?* San Diego, CA: ReferencePoint, 2014. Print.

Websites

To learn more about Essential Issues, visit **booklinks.abdopublishing.com**. These links are routinely monitored and updated to provide the most current information available.

For More Information

For more information on this subject, contact or visit the following organizations:

The National Campaign to Prevent Teen and Unplanned Pregnancy
1776 Massachusetts Avenue, NW, Suite 200
Washington, DC 20036
202-478-8500
http://www.thenationalcampaign.org
The National Campaign to Prevent Teen and Unplanned Pregnancy works to improve the lives of all by helping prevent teen and unplanned pregnancy.

Planned Parenthood
434 West Thirty-Third Street
New York, NY 10001
212-541-7800
http://www.plannedparenthood.org
Planned Parenthood provides health care and sex education to millions worldwide.

SOURCE NOTES

Chapter 1. Kids Having Kids

1. "Interview with Taylor Yoxheimer, 18." *The Candie's Foundation.* The Candie's Foundation, 2013. Web. 28 Nov. 2013.

2. "Teen Pregnancy." *Stayteen.org.* The National Campaign to Prevent Teen and Unplanned Pregnancy, 2013. Web. 28 Nov. 2013.

3. Ibid.

4. "Teen Pregnancy Prevention." *NCSL.* National Conference of State Legislatures, 2013. Web. 29 Nov. 2013.

5. Ibid.

6. Susan Dudley. "Teenage Women, Abortion, and the Law." *NAF.* National Abortion Federation, 2010. Web. 29 Nov. 2013.

7. Brady E. Hamilton and Stephanie J. Ventura. "Birth Rates for US Teenagers Reach Historic Lows for All Age and Ethnic Groups." *CDC.* Centers for Disease Control and Prevention, 10 Apr. 2012. Web. 29 Nov. 2013.

8. "Demographic Yearbook." *United Nations Statistics Division.* United Nations, 2013. Web. 28 Nov. 2013.

9. "Quick Facts on Teen and Unplanned Pregnancy and Birth." *The National Campaign to Prevent Teen and Unplanned Pregnancy.* The National Campaign to Prevent Teen and Unplanned Pregnancy, 2013. Web. 27 Nov. 2013.

10. "Teen Pregnancy." *Stayteen.org.* The National Campaign to Prevent Teen and Unplanned Pregnancy, 2013. Web. 28 Nov. 2013.

11. Ibid.

12. Ibid.

13. "Adolescent Pregnancy." *World Health Organization.* WHO, 2013. Web. 28 Nov. 2013.

14. Ibid.

15. Ibid.

16. "World Report on Violence and Health." *World Health Organization.* WHO, 2013. Web. 25 Nov. 2013.

Chapter 2. Changing Views on Teen Pregnancy

1. Heather Boonstra. "Teen Pregnancy: Trends and Lessons Learned." *Guttmacher Institute.* Guttmacher Institute, Feb. 2002. Web. 28 Nov. 2013.

2. Desirae M. Domenico and Karen H. Jones. "Adolescent Pregnancy in America: Causes and Responses." *The Journal for Vocational Special Needs Education* 30.1 (2007): 5. Web.

3. "Forced to Give Up Their Babies." *People* 66.12 (2006): 159–164. Web.

4. "Roe v. Wade: Its History and Impact." *Planned Parenthood.* Planned Parenthood Federation of America, 2013. Web. 27 Nov. 2013.

Chapter 3. Why Do Teens Get Pregnant?

1. "Adolescent Sexual Health in Europe and the US." *Advocates for Youth.* Advocates for Youth, 2008. Web. 24 Nov. 2013.

2. "Contraception." *CDC.* Centers for Disease Control and Prevention, 28 Aug. 2013. Web. 24 Nov. 2013.

3. Michelle Castillo. "Unplanned Pregnancies 20 Times More Likely on Birth Control Pill than IUD, Study Finds." *CBSNews.* CBS Interactive Inc., 24 May 2012. Web. 26 Nov. 2013.

4. Bruce J. Ellis, et al. "Does Father Absence Place Daughters at Special Risk for Early Sexual Activity and Teenage Pregnancy?" *NCBI*. National Center for Biotechnology Information, n.d. Web. 24 Nov. 2013.

5. Sara Leonard, et al. "Help Me to Succeed." *The National Campaign to Prevent Teen Pregnancy and the GCAPP*. Georgia Campaign for Adolescent Power and Potential, 2011. Web. 25 Nov. 2013.

6. Ibid.

7. Jay G. Silverman, et al. "Dating Violence and Associated Sexual Risk and Pregnancy Among Adolescent Girls in the United States." *Pediatrics*. American Academy of Pediatrics, 2013. Web. 26 Nov. 2013.

8. "Fast Facts." *The National Campaign to Prevent Teen and Unplanned Pregnancy*. The National Campaign to Prevent Teen and Unplanned Pregnancy, 2013. Web. 27 Nov. 2013.

9. Amy Kramer. "Girl Talk: What High School Senior Girls Have to Say about Sex, Love, and Relationships." *The National Campaign to Prevent Teen and Unplanned Pregnancy*. The National Campaign to Prevent Teen and Unplanned Pregnancy, 2012. Web. 29 Nov. 2013.

10. "The Sexual Attitudes and Behavior of Male Teens." *The National Campaign to Prevent Teen and Unplanned Pregnancy*. The National Campaign to Prevent Teen and Unplanned Pregnancy, 2003. Web. 27 Nov. 2013.

11. "Sex and Tech." *The National Campaign to Prevent Teen and Unplanned Pregnancy*. The National Campaign to Prevent Teen and Unplanned Pregnancy, 2008. Web. 27 Nov. 2013.

Chapter 4. Tough Choices

1. "Trends in Teen Pregnancy and Childbearing." *Office of Adolescent Health*. Office of Adolescent Health, 20 Dec. 2013. Web. 27 Nov. 2013.

2. Alison Stewart Ng and Kelleen Kaye. "Teen Childbearing, Single Parenthood, and Father Involvement." *The National Campaign to Prevent Teen and Unplanned Pregnancy*. The National Campaign to Prevent Teen and Unplanned Pregnancy, Oct. 2012. Web. 27 Nov. 2013.

3. Ibid.

4. Sarah Kershaw. "Now, the Bad News on Teenage Marriage." *New York Times*. New York Times, 3 Sept. 2008. Web. 28 Nov. 2013.

5. Ibid.

6. Sharon Jayson. "Does 'Juno' Show Strength or Glorify Teen Pregnancy?" *ABC News*. ABC News Internet Ventures,10 Mar. 2008. Web. 27 Nov. 2013.

Chapter 5. Teen Moms

1. "Trends in Teen Pregnancy and Childbearing." *Office of Adolescent Health*. Office of Adolescent Health, 20 Dec. 2013. Web. 27 Nov. 2013.

2. Mike Berry. "A Day in the Life of a Teen Mom." *Orlando Sentinel*. Orlando Sentinel, 17 Dec. 1996. Web. 28 Nov. 2013.

3. "Pregnant and Parenting Unaccompanied Youth." *National Network for Youth*. National Network for Youth, n.d. Web. 28 Nov. 2013.

4. Neal Karlinsky and Jessica Hopper. "Washington Teen Gaby Rodriguez, 17, Fakes Pregnancy as Social Experiment." *ABC News*. ABC News Internet Ventures, 22 Apr. 2011. Web. 27 Nov. 2013.

5. Naiyereh Najati and Morteza Gojazadeh. "Maternal and Neonatal Complications in Mothers Aged Under 18 Years." *NCBI*. National Center for Biotechnology Information, 21 July 2010. Web. 26 Nov. 2013.

SOURCE NOTES CONTINUED

6. "Teen Pregnancy and Other Health Issues." *The National Campaign to Prevent Teen and Unplanned Pregnancy*. The National Campaign to Prevent Teen and Unplanned Pregnancy, n.d. Web. 27 Nov. 2013.

7. Charles E. Basch. "Teen Pregnancy and the Achievement Gap among Urban Minority Youth." *Journal of School Health* 81.10 (2011): 614–618. Web. 24 Nov. 2013.

8. Saul D. Hoffman and Rebecca Maynard, eds. *Kids Having Kids: Economic Costs and Social Consequences of Teen Pregnancy*. Washington DC: Urban Institute, 2008. Print. 362.

9. "Teen Pregnancy, Poverty, and Income Disparity." *The National Campaign to Prevent Teen and Unplanned Pregnancy*. The National Campaign to Prevent Teen and Unplanned Pregnancy, Mar. 2010. Web. 26 Nov. 2013.

10. Ibid.

11. Mark Lino. "Expenditures on Children by Families, 2012." *US Department of Agriculture*. US Department of Agriculture, Aug. 2013. Web. 24 Nov. 2013.

Chapter 6. Teen Dads

1. Mamta Badkar and Elif Ince. "Doing This by Yourself." *Bronx Ink*. Bronx Ink, 19 June 2010. Web. 28 Nov. 2013.

2. Kathleen Teltsch. "Reaching Out to Unwed Teen-Age Fathers." *New York Times*. New York Times Company, 7 Oct. 1985. Web. 28 Nov. 2013.

3. Jason M. Fletcher and Barbara L. Wolfe. "The Effects of Teenage Fatherhood on Young Adult Outcomes." *Economic Inquiry* 50.1 (2012): 182–201. Web.

4. Stephen Caesar. "Children's Hospital L.A. Program Reaches Out to Teen Dads." *Los Angeles Times*. Los Angeles Times, 13 July 2013. Web. 24 Nov. 2013.

5. Mindy E. Scott, et al. "The Characteristics and Circumstances of Teen Fathers." *Child Trends*. Child Trends, June 2012. Web. 29 Nov. 2013.

6. Alison Stewart Ng and Kelleen Kaye. "Teen Childbearing, Single Parenthood, and Father Involvement." *The National Campaign to Prevent Teen and Unplanned Pregnancy*. The National Campaign to Prevent Teen and Unplanned Pregnancy, Oct. 2012. Web. 27 Nov. 2013.

7. Ibid.

8. Ibid.

Chapter 7. Children of Teens

1. Saul D. Hoffman and Rebecca Maynard, eds. *Kids Having Kids: Economic Costs and Social Consequences of Teen Pregnancy*. Washington DC: Urban Institute, 2008. Print. 362.

2. "Teen Pregnancy and Education." *The National Campaign to Prevent Teen and Unplanned Pregnancy*. The National Campaign to Prevent Teen and Unplanned Pregnancy, n.d. Web. 26 Nov. 2013.

3. Saul D. Hoffman. "By the Numbers: The Public Costs of Teen Childbearing." *The National Campaign to Prevent Teen and Unplanned Pregnancy*. The National Campaign to Prevent Teen and Unplanned Pregnancy, 2006. Web. 27 Nov. 2013.

4. Ibid.

5. "Teen Pregnancy and Child Welfare." *The National Campaign to Prevent Teen and Unplanned Pregnancy*. The National Campaign to Prevent Teen and Unplanned Pregnancy, n.d. Web. 26 Nov. 2013.

6. Saul D. Hoffman and Rebecca Maynard, eds. *Kids Having Kids: Economic Costs and Social Consequences of Teen Pregnancy*. Washington DC: Urban Institute, 2008. Print. 261–262.

7. Saul D. Hoffman. "By the Numbers: The Public Costs of Teen Childbearing." *The National Campaign to Prevent Teen and Unplanned Pregnancy*. The National Campaign to Prevent Teen and Unplanned Pregnancy, 2006. Web. 27 Nov. 2013.

8. Ibid.

9. "Teen Childbearing Cost Taxpayers $10.9 Billion in 2008." *PR Newswire*. PR Newswire Association LLC, 9 June 2011. Web. 26 Nov. 2013.

10. Heather D. Boonstra. "Teen Pregnancy among Young Women in Foster Care: A Primer." *Guttmacher Institute*. Guttmacher Institute, 2011. Web. 25 Nov. 2013.

11. "Teen Pregnancy Prevention." *NCSL*. National Conference of State Legislatures, 2013. Web. 29 Nov. 2013.

12. "Counting It Up: The Public Costs of Teen Childbearing." *The National Campaign to Prevent Teen and Unplanned Pregnancy*. The National Campaign to Prevent Teen and Unplanned Pregnancy, n.d. Web. 26 Nov. 2013.

Chapter 8. A Global Issue

1. Nancy Williamson. "Motherhood in Childhood." *Save the Children*. Save the Children, 2013. Web. 27 Nov. 2013.

2. Ibid.

3. "Child Marriages: 39,000 Every Day." *World Health Organization*. WHO, 7 Mar. 2013. Web. 28 Nov. 2013.

4. Ibid.

5. Nancy Williamson. "Motherhood in Childhood." *Save the Children*. Save the Children, 2013. Web. 27 Nov. 2013.

6. Ibid.

7. Ibid.

8. Ibid.

9. Mereso Kilusu. "Married at 13 to Man in His 70s: Child Bride Who's Changing Attitudes." *CNN*. Cable News Network, 8 Mar. 2013. Web. 27 Nov. 2013.

10. Nancy Williamson. "Motherhood in Childhood." *Save the Children*. Save the Children, 2013. Web. 27 Nov. 2013.

11. Ibid.

12. Ibid.

13. Ibid.

14. Ibid.

Chapter 9. Teen Pregnancy Prevention

1. Julie Nelson. "Teen Pregnancy: Young Girls Wanting a Baby." *Kare11*. Multimedia KARE, Inc., 14 May 2010. Web. 28 Nov. 2013.

2. Bill Albert. "With One Voice 2012: America's Adults and Teens Sound Off about Teen Pregnancy." *The National Campaign to Prevent Teen and Unplanned Pregnancy*. The National Campaign to Prevent Teen and Unplanned Pregnancy, Dec. 2012. Web. 29 Nov. 2013.

3. Ibid.

4. Carmen Solomon-Fears. "Teenage Pregnancy Prevention: Statistics and Programs." Information Resource Center. *Information Resource Center*, 19 June 2013. Web. 27 Nov. 2013.

5. Theresa Tamkins. "Virginity Pledges Don't Mean Much, Study Says." *CNN*. Cable News Network, 30 Dec. 2008. Web. 29 Nov. 2013.

INDEX

ABOUT THE AUTHOR

Karen Latchana Kenney is an author and editor from Minneapolis, Minnesota. She has written more than 80 educational books about issues such as illegal immigration and domestic violence. Her books have received positive reviews in *Booklist*, *Library Media Connection*, and *School Library Journal*.

ABOUT THE CONSULTANT

Dr. Carl Mazza is the founder and former director of the Young Fathers Program at Louis Wise Services in New York, New York. The Young Fathers Program was one of the first teen fathers programs in NYC. Dr. Mazza has worked with adolescent parents for decades and has written extensively on the subject of teen fathers. He is a frequent lecturer on adolescent parenting and fatherhood.